About the Author™

Meet
Paula Danziger

WITHDRAWN

Frances E. Ruffin

The Rosen Publishing Group's
PowerKids Press™

For Nita and Art, and for their girls, Annie and Jenny Ampat, and Juanita Fountain

Published in 2006 by The Rosen Publishing Group, Inc.
29 East 21st Street, New York, NY 10010

First Edition

Editor: Rachel O'Connor
Book Design: Julio A. Gil
Photo Researcher: Cindy Reiman

Photo Credits: Cover, title page, p. 20 Photos © Sigrid Estrada; pp. 4, 22 commissioned by Reed Children's Books, UK; pp. 8, 12 © Bettmann/Corbis; p. 11 Courtesy of Garry Rideout; p. 15 © Bryan F. Peterson/Corbis; p. 16 Cindy Reiman; p. 21 © Howard Dratch/The Image Works

Grateful acknowledgment is made for permission to reprint previously published material:
pp. 6 (illustration), 7 From AMBER BROWN IS NOT A CRAYON by Paula Danziger, illustrated by Tony Ross, copyright © 1994 by Tony Ross, illustrations. Used by permission of G.P. Putnam's Sons, A Division of Penguin Young Readers Group, A Member of Penguin Group (USA) Inc., 345 Hudson Street, New York, NY 10014. All rights reserved.
p. 6 (text) From AMBER BROWN IS NOT A CRAYON by Paula Danziger, copyright © 1994 by Paula Danziger, text. Used by permission of G.P. Putnam's Sons, A Division of Penguin Young Readers Group, A Member of Penguin Group (USA) Inc., 345 Hudson Street, New York, NY 10014. All rights reserved.
p. 14 From THE PISTACHIO PRESCRIPTION by Paula Danziger. Text copyright © 1978 by Paula Danziger. Used by permission of PaperStar, A Division of Penguin Young Readers Group, A Member of Penguin Group (USA) Inc., 345 Hudson Street, New York, NY 10014. All rights reserved.
p. 17 From THE CAT ATE MY GYMSUIT by Paula Danziger, copyright © 1974 by Paula Danziger, text. Used by permission of G.P. Putnam's Sons, A Division of Penguin Young Readers Group, A Member of Penguin Group (USA) Inc., 345 Hudson Street, New York, NY 10014. All rights reserved.
pp. 18, 19 From THERE'S A BAT IN BUNK FIVE by Paula Danziger, copyright © 1980 by Paula Danziger. Used by permission of PaperStar, A Division of Penguin Young Readers Group, A Member of Penguin Group (USA) Inc., 345 Hudson Street, New York, NY 10014. All rights reserved.
p. 22 (text) "Top Ten Tips for Anyone Who wants to be a writer" by Paula Danziger from Scholastic.com

Library of Congress Cataloging-in-Publication Data

Ruffin, Frances E.
  Meet Paula Danziger / Frances E. Ruffin.
     v. cm. — (About the author)
  Includes index.
  Contents: Writing with a funny bone — Family life – Books and comedy — College and a mentor — The students' teacher — Accidents strike — First book — Writing full-time — A sad good bye — In her own words.
  ISBN 1-4042-3133-1 (library binding)
  1. Danziger, Paula, 1944– —Juvenile literature. 2. Authors, American—20th century—Biography—Juvenile literature. I. Title. II. Series.
  PS3554.A585Z86 2006
  813'.54—dc22

                        2005002886

Manufactured in the United States of America

Contents

When writers got together at conferences, or meetings, Paula Danziger could be easily spotted among her fellow writers. She was the woman who wore colorful clothes, a lot of jewelry, and shiny shoes.

Writing with a Funny Bone

Paula Danziger is the creator of the Amber Brown series. Amber Brown is one of the most popular third graders in children's **literature**. Paula is also the voice behind such middle-school and high-school heroines as Marcy in *The Cat Ate My Gymsuit* and Phoebe in *The Divorce Express*. These characters **survive** low **self-esteem** and **peer pressure**. They also have families that do not function, or work, well. Amber and the other characters use **humor** to survive it all, as Paula did in her own life. It has been said that part of the secret of Paula's success is that she had the gift of looking at the world through the eyes of a 13- or 14-year-old.

Paula knew that she wanted to be a writer when she was in the second grade. She had what she called a magic pencil and a magic eraser. She used the pencil to create an imaginary town and the people who lived in it. She erased what she didn't like. It's what she said she did later as a writer.

Family Life

"It's not easy choosing a new best friend. . . . First of all, it's going to take a long time to decide and then what if the person I choose already has a best friend or doesn't want me as a best friend."

—From p. 62, Amber Brown Is Not a Crayon

Paula Danziger was born in Washington, D.C., on August 18, 1944. She grew up in Metuchen, New Jersey. Paula's father was a salesman, and her mother was a nurse. She had one brother, Barry, who was three years younger than she was.

Paula's family life was hard. Her father was often angry and he would yell at his family. Paula's father even yelled at her when she showed that she was good at something. Paula made sure that she kept a C average in school, so her father would not be angry with her. Paula described her mother as weak and unable to stand up to him.

There are nine books in the Amber Brown series. All of the books deal with real-life issues, such as divorce, homework, making friends, and getting your ears pierced! The first book, *Amber Brown Is Not a Crayon*, is about Amber's feelings of loss when her best friend moves away.

In her first book, The Cat Ate My Gymsuit, Paula named the main character Marcy Lewis. The "Lewis" is for Jerry Lewis, Paula's favorite comedian.

Books and Comedy

Books and her love of reading helped Paula survive her unhappy childhood. Her favorite memories include being left at the public library to read while her mother shopped. Paula was usually seen with a book under her arm. By the time she was in second grade, Paula knew that she wanted to be a writer.

Books were not the only things that helped Paula live through her teenage years. **Comedy** helped, too. Having to deal with family problems made her a sad and angry teenager. However, she found that comedy could help take away the pain. As other kids her age became fans of rock stars, Paula fell in love with the comedians of the 1950s, such as Jerry Lewis.

As a young child, Paula liked to read the book The Little Engine That Could. As an adult before making a speech or going on television, she would say to herself the Little Engine's lines, "I think I can, I think I can, I know I can." As an older child, she read Little Women, A Tree Grows in Brooklyn, and the Nancy Drew and Hardy Boys series.

A Friend and a Mentor

When she finished high school, Paula earned a **scholarship** to New Jersey's Montclair State Teacher's College. She failed her earth science course and gym, but she was the editor of *Galumph*, a college humor magazine. She **graduated** from Montclair State with a **degree** in English in 1967.

During college Paula earned money by babysitting the children of poet John Ciardi. Paula became part of the Ciardi family, spending holidays with them. Most important, John Ciardi served as a mentor, or teacher, to Paula. He **encouraged** her to believe in herself and her talent as a writer. He taught her to see how language is used in poetry. This helped Paula in her writing.

Paula's mentor, John Ciardi, once had her read a poem and underline the funny lines in red and the serious lines in blue. By the time she was finished, the poem was underlined in purple. Paula said that life is funny and serious at the same time. Her stories also blur, or mix, the line between the funny and the serious.

Paula applied to Montclair State University, shown here, as a sort of dare. One of her high-school teachers had told her she would not get in. To prove the teacher wrong, Paula applied and got in!

Paula once had students make a bulletin board using Martin Luther King Jr.'s words, "We must live together as brothers or perish as fools." "Perish" means to die.

The Students' Teacher

In 1967, Paula began a **career** teaching English. She taught eighth- and ninth-grade students. She was very popular with her students. Paula hardly ever had a lesson plan because she preferred to **improvise** what she taught each day. Once to make a point, Paula brought in a 6-foot (1.8 m) movie poster of actor-director Woody Allen. Paula also taught how children of different races can get along, using the poems of African American poet Langston Hughes and the words of Martin Luther King Jr. Her students loved her classes, and they all learned a lot. Students in her classes who did not like to read at the beginning of the year usually loved books by the end of it.

In her lifetime Paula wrote more than 25 books for young readers and won several awards for them. The awards include the 1980 Children's Choice Award given by the International Reading Association and the Children's Book Council.

13

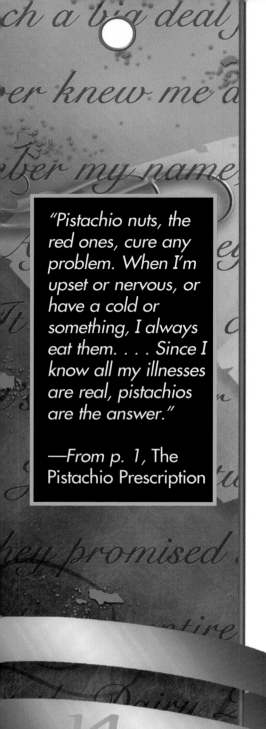

> "Pistachio nuts, the red ones, cure any problem. When I'm upset or nervous, or have a cold or something, I always eat them. . . . Since I know all my illnesses are real, pistachios are the answer."
>
> —From p. 1, The Pistachio Prescription

Accidents Strike

In April 1970, two **accidents** occurred in the space of a week that completely changed Paula's life. While Paula was stopped at a stop sign, a police car accidentally ran into the back of her car. The accident gave her whiplash, a painful **injury** to her neck. A few days later, a drunk driver hit Paula's car head-on. Luckily she was wearing a seat belt. However, her injuries from this accident were more serious than those from the first. She had to have more than 100 **stitches** in her head and face. She also suffered some harm to her brain, which had an effect on her ability to walk, read, and write.

At the time of the accidents, Paula had recently returned to Montclair State University to earn a higher degree called a masters. However, the accident at the stop sign and the one that followed put her studies and teaching on hold.

Marcy Lewis is the heroine of The Cat Ate My Gymsuit. Even though Marcy is overweight and her family life is hard, Paula tells her story with humor and tenderness.

First Book

To help get healthy again, Paula had **physical therapy**. This helped her body heal. She began to see a **psychologist** to help heal her mind. While seeing the psychologist, Paula began to write again. Four years after the accidents, she published her first book, *The Cat Ate My Gymsuit*, in 1974. This is her most personal book. As Paula was as a child, Marcy is a chubby girl who hates school, especially gym. The title comes from one of the many excuses Marcy uses to get out of taking gym. As Paula did, Marcy has a father who yells a lot. It took Paula three years to write the book. It was immediately popular with middle-school students.

"She was young and pretty and seemed nice. She sounded smart. She was different, but I wasn't sure how, and I didn't know if I could trust her. I mean, she was a teacher, and an adult."

—From pp. 8–9, The Cat Ate My Gymsuit

Writing Full-time

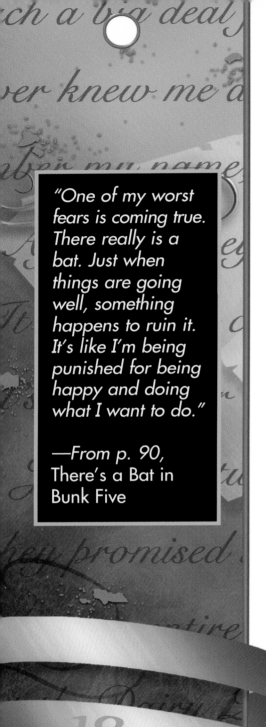

In 1978, Paula quit teaching. That same year she **published** *The Pistachio Prescription*. Paula told the story through the eyes of 13-year-old Cassie Stephens. In the story Cassie is hard on her parents, who are having problems in their marriage.

When Paula's book *Can You Sue Your Parents for **Malpractice**?* was published in 1979, Paula considered herself to be a full-time writer. In addition to writing books for children, Paula started another career as a public speaker. It came out of her enjoyment of being onstage. She was invited to speak before many different kinds of groups around the world.

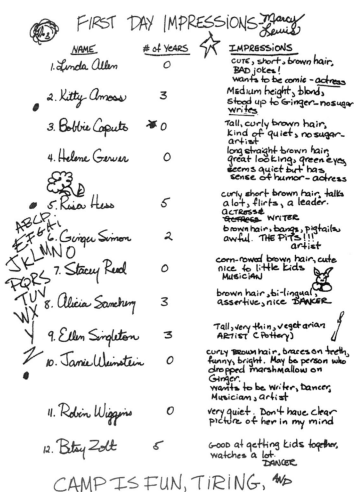

FIRST DAY IMPRESSIONS — Marcy Lewis

NAME	# of YEARS	IMPRESSIONS
1. Linda Allen	0	cute, short, brown hair, BAD jokes! wants to be comic - actress
2. Kitty Amoss	3	Medium height, blond, stood up to Ginger - no sugar WRITES
3. Bobbie Caputo	0	Tall, curly brown hair, kind of quiet, no sugar - artist
4. Helene Gerver	0	long straight brown hair, great looking, green eyes seems quiet but has sense of humor - actress
5. Rina Hess	5	curly short brown hair, talks a lot, flirts, a leader. ACTRESS WRITER
6. Ginger Simon	2	brown hair, bangs, pigtails, awful. THE PITS!!! artist
7. Stacey Reed	0	corn-rowed brown hair, cute nice to little kids MUSICIAN
8. Alicia Sanchez	3	brown hair, bi-lingual, assertive, nice DANCER
9. Ellen Singleton	3	Tall, very thin, vegetarian ARTIST (Pottery)
10. Janie Weinstein	0	curly brown hair, braces on teeth, funny, bright. May be person who dropped marshmallow on Ginger. wants to be writer, dancer, musician, artist
11. Robin Wiggins	0	very quiet. Don't have clear picture of her in my mind
12. Betsy Zolt	5	Good at getting kids together, watches a lot. DANCER

ABCD
EFGH
JKLMNO
PQRS
TUV
WX
Y
Z

CAMP IS FUN, TIRING, AND CONFUSING!

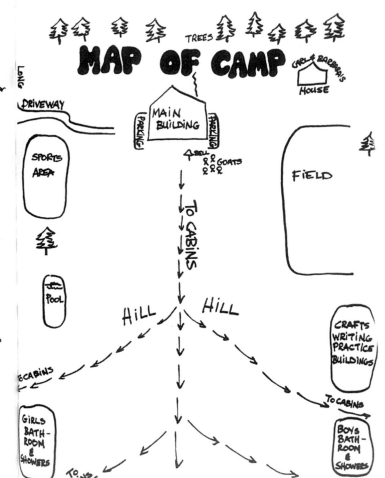

MAP OF CAMP

TREES

CARL & BARBARA'S HOUSE

DRIVEWAY

PARKING — MAIN BUILDING — PARKING

LONG

SPORTS AREA

GOATS

FIELD

TO CABINS

POOL

HILL   HILL

TO CABINS   TO CABINS

CRAFTS WRITING PRACTICE BUILDINGS

GIRLS BATHROOM & SHOWERS

BOYS BATHROOM & SHOWERS

TO CABINS

There's a Bat in Bunk Five continues to tell the story of Marcy Lewis. In this book Marcy is away at camp for the summer. During her first day there, she draws a map of the camp and writes down her opinions of the other girls.

In her career as a public speaker, Paula spoke to college students, business people, and writers at writers' conferences. Paula was a funny, warm, and wise speaker. People loved to hear her talk about her life and what it was like to be a writer.

A Sad Good-bye

Over her lifetime Paula became a successful writer and speaker. She loved to see the world and traveled up to 50,000 miles (80,467 km) a year for business and for pleasure. When she was at home, she stayed at her New York City apartment, her London apartment, or her country home in Woodstock, New York.

Paula enjoyed her success and shared it with everyone close to her. It came as a great sadness when Paula Danziger died of a heart attack on July 8, 2004. She had never married or had children. However, her literary children, including Amber Brown, Marcy Lewis, and Cassie Stephens will live on in the hearts and minds of millions of young readers around the world.

Paula liked to spend time writing when she was in Woodstock.

21

In Her Own Words

Here are 10 tips from Paula for anyone who wants to be a writer:

1. Read as much as you can.

2. Write and rewrite.

3. Read your work aloud.

4. Let trusted people look at your work and offer suggestions.

5. Take acting lessons. (It will teach you a lot about building characters.)

6. Observe people.

7. Eavesdrop, or listen in on people's conversations.

8. Don't be afraid of not being perfect.

9. Remember, the most important thing you can create is the kind of person you are and become.

10. Don't eat tuna fish salad with mayo if it's been out in the sun too long.

Glossary

accidents (AK-seh-dents) Unexpected and sometimes bad events.

career (kuh-REER) Job.

comedy (KAH-meh-dee) Something funny.

degree (dih-GREE) A title given to a person who has finished a course of study.

encouraged (in-KUR-ijd) Gave someone reason to do something.

graduated (GRA-jeh-wayt-ed) To have finished a course of school.

humor (HYOO-mer) Being funny.

improvise (IM-pruh-vyz) To act without preparation.

injury (INJ-ree) Physical harm or hurt done to a person.

literature (LIH-tuh-ruh-chur) Writings such as books, plays, and poetry.

malpractice (mal-PRAK-tes) Illegal or improper behavior.

peer pressure (PEER PREH-shur) Friends or classmates making you feel like you have to do something you do not want to do.

physical therapy (FIH-zih-kul THEHR-uh-pee) Exercises to heal the body.

psychologist (sy-KAH-luh-jist) A person who is trained to study the mind and behavior.

published (PUH-blishd) Printed so that people can read it.

scholarship (SKAH-ler-ship) Money given to someone to pay for school.

self-esteem (self-uh-STEEM) Happiness with oneself.

stitches (STICH-ez) The thread left in the skin after a needle is passed in and out to close a cut.

survive (sur-VYV) To live through.

23

Index

Web Sites

Due to the changing nature of Internet links, PowerKids Press has developed an online list of Web sites related to the subject of this book. This site is updated regularly. Please use this link to access the list: www.powerkidslinks.com/aa/pauladanz/